DEALING WITH
**MENTAL
DISORDERS**

DEALING WITH

PSYCHOTIC
DISORDERS

By Marie-Therese Miller, Ph. D.

*Reference*Point
Press®

San Diego, CA

© 2020 ReferencePoint Press, Inc.
Printed in the United States

For more information, contact:
ReferencePoint Press, Inc.
PO Box 27779
San Diego, CA 92198
www.ReferencePointPress.com

Content Consultant: Carla Marie Manly, PhD

LIBRARY OF CONGRESS CATALOGING-IN-PUBLICATION DATA

Names: Miller, Marie-Therese, author.
Title: Dealing with psychotic disorders / Marie-Therese Miller, Ph. D.
Description: San Diego, CA : ReferencePoint Press, [2020] | Series: Dealing with mental
  disorders | Includes bibliographical references and index. | Audience: Grades 10-12
Identifiers: LCCN 2019034014 (print) | LCCN 2019034015 (eBook) | ISBN 9781682827932
  (hardcover) | ISBN 9781682827949 (eBook)
Subjects: LCSH: Psychoses. | Psychoses--Treatment. | Psychoses in adolescence.
Classification: LCC RC512 .M55 2020 (print) | LCC RC512 (ebook) | DDC 616.89--dc23
LC record available at https://lccn.loc.gov/2019034014
LC ebook record available at https://lccn.loc.gov/2019034015

CONTENTS

LOSING TOUCH
WITH REALITY

The sun was warm on Ella's shoulders, but the breeze carried the suggestion of the cooler autumn weather to come. She was excited to begin graduate school. She would be studying English at the university and dreamed of becoming a novelist. Ella grabbed some moving boxes and carried them up the front steps of the one-bedroom apartment she had rented off campus. She unpacked the boxes, folding her clothes and tucking them in the dresser and stacking dishes in the kitchen cabinets.

When she finished, she sat down. Suddenly, she felt alone. She missed her parents and her poodle, Oreo. She had left the dog with her family. It was the right thing to do because he was old and needed the full-time care and attention they could give him. Even still, she was sad without him.

The schoolwork was challenging. The professors assigned loads of reading and long papers. Ella struggled to get everything done. Her professors appreciated her writing skills, though, and she earned good grades. Ella went home for the holiday break to de-stress. When she

Early signs of psychosis may include trouble reading or concentrating. Talking about such symptoms with medical professionals is important.

returned for the spring semester, she started having trouble concentrating on the class readings. She would have to read paragraphs over and over again. She handed in her papers after the due dates—if she even finished them at all.

On February 10, her mom called to tell her that Oreo was sick. Ella was terribly worried about the dog. The next day, her dad called to let her know that Oreo had died. Ella cried for hours. She began to believe that her anxious thoughts about his health had somehow caused Oreo's death. All she could think about was Oreo. She stopped sleeping. She could hardly eat.

One afternoon while walking though the university parking lot, she spotted a license plate that read "ORO2424." She was convinced that the license plate was a message sent to her from Oreo. He was reaching out to her from the afterlife. Gradually, Ella stopped attending classes. She spent her time wandering the campus searching for signs from Oreo. Sometimes, she thought Oreo sent other dogs or cats to communicate with her. Eventually, she heard Oreo talking directly to her. Once in a while, she even saw him lying on the foot of her bed.

Late one night, she phoned her mom. Ella was talking so much and so quickly that her mother couldn't get a word in edgewise. "Oreo ordered me to quit school and become a pet psychic," Ella announced. "Oreo will tell me how to help other people and their pets. I will be the most famous pet psychic in the world."

Ella's parents rushed up to the university. They were shocked when they entered her apartment and saw dirty clothes in piles. Ella looked as if she hadn't showered in weeks. She had dark circles under her eyes, and she was too thin. They convinced her to go to the hospital emergency room. There, the emergency room doctor ordered blood and urine tests and a magnetic resonance imaging (MRI) scan of her brain. All the tests came back negative for medical problems.

A psychiatrist met with Ella. He diagnosed her with psychosis and administered the antipsychotic medication paliperidone. He encouraged Ella to remain in the psychiatric ward of the hospital for a few weeks. She agreed. Over time, Ella was diagnosed with schizoaffective disorder, bipolar type, and she was prescribed lithobid to stabilize her mood in addition to the antipsychotic medication.

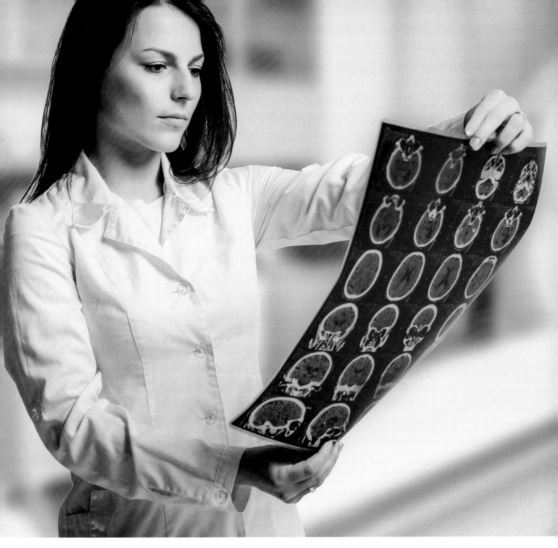

Scans of the brain, along with other tests, can help rule out some causes of psychosis. This is a critical step in getting an accurate diagnosis.

Ella left graduate school for that semester. The medications helped relieve most of her hallucinations, delusions, and mood disturbances. However, she spent the rest of the spring and the summer months going to cognitive behavioral therapy to learn to cope with the delusions that remained. She also worked on improving her school skills with an education specialist. She was determined to return to graduate school in the autumn.

PSYCHOTIC DISORDERS

Schizoaffective disorder is a type of psychotic disorder. Psychotic disorders have psychosis as a symptom. Psychosis is a general term to describe certain symptoms of mental illness that result in highly abnormal thinking, speech, perceptions, behaviors, and emotions. People who have psychosis perceive things that are not rooted in what is actually happening around them. Psychosis occurs in psychotic disorders, but it can also be a symptom of a medical disease, a prescribed medication, or illicit drug or alcohol use.

The Diagnostic and Statistical Manual of Mental Disorders, Fifth Edition (DSM-5) is a publication put out by the American Psychiatric Association. Published in 2013 and written by international experts, it lists mental disorders and defines the symptoms of each. It has nine categories for the diagnosis of psychotic disorders.

The most common of these psychotic disorders is schizophrenia. According to the National Institute of Mental Health (NIMH), "Estimates of the prevalence of schizophrenia and related psychotic disorders in the U.S. range between 0.25% and 0.64%."[1] The incidence of schizophrenia is higher among men than women. The World Health Organization (WHO) estimates the worldwide incidence of schizophrenia at approximately 12 million men and 9 million women. Men are most often diagnosed in their late teens to early twenties, whereas women are usually diagnosed in their mid-twenties to early thirties.

> "Estimates of the prevalence of schizophrenia and related psychotic disorders in the U.S. range between 0.25% and 0.64%."[1]
>
> *– National Institute of Mental Health (NIMH)*

Schizoaffective disorder is another of the psychotic disorders. Its prevalence is 0.3 percent. There is a greater incidence of schizoaffective disorder among women than men, partly because women are diagnosed in greater numbers with a type of the disorder that is connected to depression.

Medical professionals and researchers have learned a great deal about the possible causes and risk factors for psychotic disorders. They have catalogued the symptoms of each psychotic disorder, determined how best to diagnose the disorders, and studied what it is like to live with a psychotic disorder. They have developed evidence-based treatments for helping people who have been diagnosed.

CHAPTER
ONE

WHAT ARE PSYCHOTIC DISORDERS?

Most mental health professionals rely on the *DSM-5* to categorize and diagnose psychotic disorders. There are several psychotic disorders found in the *DSM-5* under a disorder class called schizophrenia spectrum and other psychotic disorders. They include schizophrenia, schizophreniform disorder, brief psychotic disorder, schizoaffective disorder, delusional disorder, psychotic disorder due to another medical condition, substance/medication-induced psychotic disorder, specified schizophrenia spectrum and other psychotic disorder, and unspecified schizophrenia spectrum and other psychotic disorder.

PSYCHOTIC DISORDERS IN THE *DSM-5*

According to the *DSM-5*, an individual with schizophrenia will have at least two of the following symptoms, and one must be from the first three symptoms listed: delusions, hallucinations, disorganized speech, grossly disorganized behavior, and negative symptoms. These symptoms can severely affect a person's work and social life. Sufferers may have

Schizophrenia's symptoms can leave a person feeling isolated and alone. This can have a significant effect on the person's relationships.

very different types and levels of symptoms. For schizophrenia to be diagnosed, some symptoms must be present for at least six months. Other potential causes of the symptoms must also be ruled out.

What are these symptoms? Delusions are false beliefs that the person does not discard even when logical evidence is provided. For example, the individual might hold to the delusion that a foreign government is stealing his thoughts. An individual with hallucinations perceives things with his senses that are not happening in reality. The person, for instance, might hear voices talking to him when no one is actually speaking. A person with disorganized speech might talk for a long time and not make any sense. An individual with grossly disorganized behavior could demonstrate strange mannerisms or repetitive movements. For example, she might walk in circles or pace. Negative behaviors are behaviors that are less than what would be seen in a healthy person. Some people might not show any emotion on their faces, for instance. They might not feel motivation to get things done. Cognitive deficits, another part of schizophrenia, can affect processes such as working memory, attention, and decision-making.

Schizophreniform disorder is another disorder on the schizophrenia spectrum. Schizophreniform disorder involves the same symptoms as schizophrenia, but the duration is shorter. Two of the following symptoms must be present, and at least one of the first three: delusions, hallucinations, disorganized speech, grossly disorganized behavior, and negative symptoms. Unlike schizophrenia, schizophreniform disorder does not have the requirement of a decline in functioning. With schizophreniform disorder, the symptoms must be evident for one month, but persist less than six months.

Brief psychotic disorder has symptoms similar to those of schizophrenia, including confusion and mood shifts. As the name suggests, the time frame of this disorder is short but severe. It begins suddenly and then ends completely once it has run its course. If the symptoms continue longer than one month, the diagnosis changes.

Schizoaffective disorder also shares symptoms with schizophrenia, except that it has an added mood component. The person might be diagnosed with schizoaffective disorder, bipolar type, which involves a manic episode, or depressive type, which involves a major depressive episode. A diagnosis of schizoaffective disorder also requires the presence of delusions or hallucinations.

Delusional disorder's major symptom is delusions that last at least one month, but the person might also have hallucinations related to the same theme as the delusions. However, hallucinations are not the most prominent psychotic feature in this disorder. Brief mood episodes may occur, too. A person with delusional disorder does not have most of the key symptoms of schizophrenia.

Psychotic disorder due to another medical condition is diagnosed when another physical illness is determined to be the cause for psychosis. Many other medical conditions can spark psychotic symptoms, such as brain tumors and temporal lobe epilepsy. Substance or

MARIJUANA USE AND PSYCHOSIS

Research has shown that using marijuana, also known as cannabis, increases the risk of developing psychosis. Antti Mustonen and coauthors conducted a Finnish study in which 6,534 people, ages 15 to 16, were followed over 30 years. Approximately 4.8 percent who used cannabis at least five times received a psychosis diagnosis as opposed to 1.7 percent of those that did not use cannabis. The researchers write, "Current evidence indicates that early onset cannabis use predates the onset of psychosis, especially among those with pre-existing vulnerability and heavier cannabis use."[1]

Studies have shown that the earlier and the heavier the use of cannabis, the higher the risk of psychotic disorder. Psychiatrist E. Fuller Torrey warns against making a causal link, however. He suggests that cannabis might not cause psychosis. Instead, those who are experiencing the early symptoms of schizophrenia, for example, might use cannabis to self-medicate.

Rajiv Radhakrishnan and coauthors present a stunning statistic: "Longitudinal studies have found that the risk of developing schizophrenia is nearly 50 percent in patients admitted for cannabis-induced psychosis."[2] All in all, these studies are important to consider, particularly for those who are vulnerable to psychotic disorder.

1. Antti Mustonen, et al., "Adolescent Cannabis Use, Baseline Prodromal Symptoms and the Risk of Psychosis," Cambridge Core, April 2018. www.cambridge.org.

2. Rajiv Radhakrishnan, et al., "Gone to Pot—A Review of the Association Between Cannabis and Psychosis," Frontiers in Psychiatry, May 22, 2014. www.ncbi.nlm.nih.gov.

medication-induced psychotic disorder is present when the psychosis is due to alcohol, illicit drugs, or prescribed medication use. For example, marijuana, stimulant, and hallucinogen use can lead to psychotic symptoms. Delusions and/or hallucinations must be present for these diagnoses, and the disturbance must cause significant impairment.

The final two psychotic disorder diagnoses in the *DSM-5* are specified schizophrenia spectrum or other psychotic disorder and unspecified schizophrenia spectrum or other psychotic disorder. They can be used when the individual's symptoms do not meet the full diagnostic criteria of the other categories. For the specified type, the diagnosing mental health professional must record the reasons the individual does not meet the criteria for other psychotic disorder categories. For the unspecified type, she may choose not to specify. For example, a doctor in an emergency room setting may have insufficient information to make a more specific diagnosis as to the type of psychotic disorder.

HISTORY OF PSYCHOTIC DISORDERS

In 1896, German psychiatrist Emil Kraepelin defined a psychotic disorder, which he called dementia praecox. It is now known as schizophrenia. He gave the illness its name because he noted patterns of symptoms that he believed mimicked an early onset of the dementia normally seen in the elderly. Kraepelin theorized a biological basis for dementia praecox. In addition, Kraepelin is credited with differentiating dementia praecox from a psychotic illness he named manic-depressive, which parallels the mental illness we now call bipolar disorder.

Unlike Kraepelin, Swiss psychiatrist Paul Eugen Bleuler did not view the disorder as related to dementia. For this reason, he renamed the illness schizophrenia in 1908. The word *schizophrenia* is derived from

Emil Kraepelin is considered one of the earliest modern psychiatrists. He developed new ways to classify mental disorders.

Greek words meaning "split mind." Bleuler wanted the name to indicate a "loosening of associations" between thought, behavior, and emotions.[2] Unfortunately, a misconception persists that those with schizophrenia have split personalities, and people often confuse schizophrenia with the rare mental illness known as dissociative identity disorder. With dissociative identity disorder, the person has two or more identities that surface periodically, leaving gaps in memory and time for the individual.

Dissociative identity disorder is normally the result of severe physical or sexual abuse that occurred in childhood. It is completely different from schizophrenia. In a 1911 book, Bleuler wrote about the "group of schizophrenias" and identified various non-psychoses and psychoses as part of a spectrum of schizophrenia.[3]

In later decades, others recognized and named specific schizophrenia spectrum psychotic disorders. Jacob Kasanin first described schizoaffective psychosis in 1933, recognizing an illness with a combination of schizophrenic and mood symptoms. In 1939, Norwegian psychiatrist Gabriel Langfeldt identified schizophreniform psychosis as a psychotic illness with a quick onset and schizophrenic symptoms.

THE LIMITS OF KNOWLEDGE ABOUT PSYCHOTIC DISORDERS

Although researchers continue to study the nature and cause of psychotic disorders, no specific causes have been uncovered for most of these psychotic disorders. However, researchers have developed theories about possible causes and correlations. More definitive answers have been found in cases where psychotic disorders are due to other medical conditions or where disorders are caused by a substance or medication.

The research into the causes and risks associated with psychotic disorders has heavily been focused on schizophrenia. In that research, other schizophrenia spectrum disorders are sometimes lumped into the category of schizophrenia. As a result, schizophrenia-based studies are the source of most knowledge about causes and risks about psychotic disorders. In their article "Psychosis Genetics: Modeling the Relationship between Schizophrenia, Bipolar Disorder, and Mixed (or 'Schizoaffective') Psychosis," psychiatrist Nick Craddock and his coauthors note the concentration on schizophrenia research and the lack of studies into other psychotic disorders, such as schizoaffective disorder. They write, "Cases with prominent mood and psychotic features have not received the same attention as schizophrenia and bipolar disorder with respect to research into treatment and pathogenesis [the origin and development of the disease]."[4] Many researchers hope future studies will give greater attention to other psychotic disorders.

> "Cases with prominent mood and psychotic features have not received the same attention as schizophrenia and bipolar disorder with respect to research into treatment and pathogenesis [the origin and development of the disease]."[4]
>
> – Psychologist Nick Craddock and coauthors

THE GENETICS OF PSYCHOTIC DISORDERS

How much does genetics influence the development of schizophrenia or other psychotic disorders? Identical twins originate from the same egg and share 100 percent of their genetic material. On the other hand, fraternal twins come from two separate eggs and share only 50 percent of their genetic material. If the cause of psychotic disorder was solely genetic, when one identical twin was diagnosed with schizophrenia, the other twin would have a 100 percent chance of also being diagnosed with schizophrenia.

Over the years, this question has been researched through twin studies. One of these studies was conducted by Ulla Kläning and coauthors, with the results published in a 2016 article. In their research, 44 sets of twins, some identical and some fraternal, were analyzed. The researchers were investigating concordance. In genetics, the term *concordance* refers to the probability that both members of a pair will

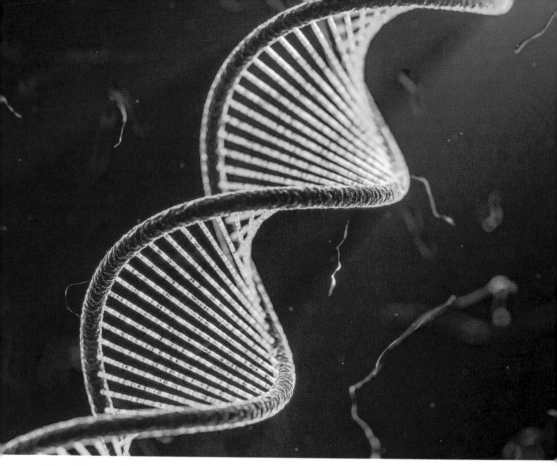

Genetics are likely a significant factor in whether a person has schizophrenia. Researchers are studying chromosomes, individual genes, and DNA to search for answers.

have a given trait or characteristic. They found that 44 percent of the identical twins were concordant for schizophrenia while only 3 percent of the fraternal twins were concordant. When the researchers broadened the criteria to all psychotic disorders, identical twins had a 50 percent concordance rate for psychotic disorders, while the fraternal twins had a 16 percent concordance rate.

This is in keeping with many of the historic twin studies that focus specifically on schizophrenia, which demonstrated a high risk for both identical twins to have the disorder. Some studies have found up to a 50 percent risk. But it is not a 100 percent risk, so genetics are not the entire story. In his book, *Surviving Schizophrenia: A Family Manual, Sixth Edition*, E. Fuller Torrey, MD, writes that identical twins share the risks of schizophrenia at about the same rate as ordinary siblings, 7 in 100. In addition, he writes that having a mother with schizophrenia creates a 9.3 in 100 risk, and having a father with schizophrenia poses a 7.2 in 100 risk.

Researchers have been hard at work searching for genes that cause psychotic disorder, particularly schizophrenia. In a 2014 article, Stephan Ripke and coauthors write about their schizophrenia genome-wide association study (GWAS). A genome is an individual's complete set of genes. In this GWAS, researchers were able to analyze a large sample of genes to determine the association of particular genes to schizophrenia. This study involved comparing 36,989 genomes from those with schizophrenia with 113,075 genomes of healthy individuals. In the end, 128 gene variants on 108 locations on the genome were found that correlate to schizophrenia.

Studies of copy number variation (CNV) are also being performed. A CNV is a mutation in which sections of the genome are deleted or duplicated. Researchers have found more CNVs in those with schizophrenia than in healthy individuals. Those with velocardiofacial syndrome, a condition that affects the shape of the face and can cause various health problems, have a large CNV deletion on one particular chromosome. Chromosomes are the structures that carry genes within cells. These individuals have a much higher risk of schizophrenia. For this reason, researchers have been studying CNVs on that chromosome.

BRAIN STRUCTURE

The brains of those with psychotic disorder can be studied through the use of brain imaging technology, such as an MRI scan, or they can be examined after death. Through such examinations, researchers have discovered structural differences in the brains of those with schizophrenia when compared to the brains of healthy people. In individuals with schizophrenia, the portions of the brain through which cerebral spinal fluid flows are enlarged. In addition, the grey matter, which contains neurons, is reduced in multiple areas, including the frontal and temporal lobes. These are areas of the brain where the higher functions, such as decision-making and language, are performed. Not surprisingly, individuals with schizophrenia often have deficits involving these types of higher brain functions.

B.L. Amann and coauthors studied the brain structures of forty-five people with schizophrenia and bipolar disorder, forty-five people with schizoaffective disorder, and forty-five healthy people. They found that those with schizoaffective disorder had a loss of gray matter similar to those with schizophrenia.

The human brain has 86 billion nerve cells known as neurons. The neurons are separated by tiny gaps called synapses. The neurons communicate with one another across the synapses electrically and chemically. Neurotransmitters are the chemicals that send messages along. The neurotransmitters travel across the nerve synapses and activate waiting proteins knows as receptors.

One of the theories about the cause of schizophrenia has to do with a process called synaptic pruning. During adolescence, the brain naturally reduces excess prefrontal gray matter that is no longer needed as it was in infancy and childhood. This is synaptic pruning. In 1983, Irwin Feinberg of the University of California theorized that in the brains of people with schizophrenia, too much of this synaptic pruning occurs. The timing of synaptic pruning coincides with the onset of schizophrenia, and the gray matter lost parallels the areas of the brain where cognitive deficits are noted in schizophrenia.

This was backed up by work done by Steve McCarroll and coauthors at the Broad Institute and Harvard Medical School. These researchers studied the gene C4. They found that people with schizophrenia are more likely to have a variant of the C4 gene, known as C4-A. They also discovered that an overexpression of C4-A caused excessive synaptic pruning.

In his book *No One Cares About Crazy People*, Ron Powers comments about the challenge of studying the abnormalities in the brains of individuals with schizophrenia.

> "Is the 'abnormality' they are looking at a *result* of schizophrenia? Or is it a *cause*?"[5]
>
> *– Writer Ron Powers on studying abnormalities in the brains of individuals with schizophrenia*

He writes, "Is the 'abnormality' they are looking at a *result* of schizophrenia? Or is it a *cause*?"[5] Researchers have to ask themselves if what they are observing is related to the cause of the psychotic disorder or is the outcome of the disease process. They even have to consider that the medications given to treat the disorder might be responsible for some of the brain differences.

Researchers who focus on the role of neurotransmitters are investigating possible connections to schizophrenia and other psychotic disorders involving the neurotransmitters dopamine, serotonin, glutamate, and GABA. Dopamine, which is involved in muscle movement and the reward system, has been of particular interest. This is because the antipsychotic medications that are effective in treating the disorders block dopamine receptors, particularly the D2 receptors. This has led researchers to theorize that either an excess of dopamine or an excess of dopamine receptors in the brain is involved. Second-generation antipsychotic medications block 5-HT receptors for serotonin, another neurotransmitter involved in the reward system. Serotonin's role in schizophrenia and other psychotic disorders is of interest to researchers as well.

ADDITIONAL RISK FACTORS

There are other risk factors that increase a person's chance of being diagnosed with schizophrenia. However, the exact reasons for the increased risks have not been determined. One interesting research finding is that immigrants moving between certain countries, such as from Jamaica to the United Kingdom and from Morocco to the Netherlands, show a 2.3 in 100 risk of developing schizophrenia. The second generations of these immigrant communities have an even greater risk of 4.5 in 100. Those who are raised in urban areas instead of rural locations have a 2.2–2.8 in 100 risk. Researchers theorize that immigrants and those who reside in urban areas might have to deal with more stress and be exposed to more illnesses, which might put them at greater risk for schizophrenia, but this has not been proven.

Other factors, such as paternal age, have been linked to an increased risk. As the age of an individual's father at the time of the individual's birth increases, the chances of the individual being diagnosed with schizophrenia increase. If the father is over 55, the risk is 2.2–5.9 in 100. If the father is over 45, the risk is 1.2–1.7 in 100. This might be because older men have more sperm cell mutations. There is a small increase in risk in people who experience birth complications, 1.3–1.4 in 100.

A person born in winter or spring and a person born when their mothers were pregnant during an influenza epidemic each have an increased risk of 1.1 in 100.

On the other hand, some populations have a lower risk. Torrey mentions that those with rheumatoid arthritis have a low incidence of schizophrenia: "Thus rheumatoid arthritis would appear to be a protective factor against schizophrenia."[6] Individuals with rheumatoid arthritis have a low incidence of schizoaffective disorder as well.

> "Rheumatoid arthritis would appear to be a protective factor against schizophrenia."[6]
>
> – *Psychiatrist E. Fuller Torrey*

AUTOIMMUNITY

Autoimmunity occurs when a person's immune system, designed to fight foreign germs in the body, turns against the person's own body by mistake. A link exists between autoimmunity and psychotic disorders. People with schizophrenia, for example, have a higher prevalence of autoimmune disorders. In autoimmune encephalitis, the immune system interferes with glutamate receptors in the brain and produces psychotic symptoms. This has ignited greater interest in the connection between autoimmunity and psychotic disorders.

Studies have shown that the immune system is more active in people with schizophrenia. These individuals have three times more of certain types of antibodies than healthy people. It has also been discovered that both schizophrenia and autoimmune disorders share a genetic association found on a particular chromosome. This new research might lead to additional options for treatment of psychotic disorders.

For example, corticosteroids, drugs that decrease the activity of the immune system, could be used for those people whose psychotic disorder has an autoimmune component.

INFECTION AND PSYCHOTIC DISORDER

There is a link between certain infections and schizophrenia. Risk increases when an individual's mother is pregnant during an influenza epidemic, particularly during the first half of pregnancy. The risk of schizophrenia is also increased in babies born in the winter or spring, times when respiratory illness and influenza are at a peak. In addition, a person infected with the common Toxoplasma gondii parasite has a 2.7 in 100 risk of having schizophrenia. Researchers are exploring the association between infection and psychotic disorders.

In his book *Infectious Behavior: Brain-Immune Connections in Autism, Schizophrenia, and Depression*, Paul H. Patterson notes that identical twins who share the same placenta, and thus the exact same prenatal environment, have a 60 percent concordance where schizophrenia is concerned. Those identical twins who do not share a placenta have only an 11 percent concordance rate. This points to the role of fetal environment rather than genetics in the development of schizophrenia.

Some experts theorize that whatever infections the mother fights might in some way affect the developing fetus in the placental environment. In fact, researchers are investigating prenatal exposure to rubella, Toxoplasma gondii, and herpes simplex virus type 2 and their possible connection to a schizophrenia diagnosis later in life.

Torrey investigated Toxoplasma gondii, which is connected to cats and found often in their litter boxes. He was fascinated to find that there were more cases of psychotic disorders being diagnosed in the United Kingdom and United States after 1871, when owning cats as house pets became popular. In his studies, Torrey notes that prenatal exposure to the parasite increases the risk of schizophrenia. But Torrey found that the strongest connections between the parasite and schizophrenia were found when the infection was contracted by children and teens. He blames Toxoplasma gondii that can be found in outdoor sandboxes for the infections in this age group.

GUT MICROBIOME, DIET, AND PSYCHOTIC DISORDERS

Many researchers are turning their attention to the microbiome in the gastrointestinal tract, or gut, and its connection to the central nervous system and, in turn, its connection to psychotic disorders. The gut microbiome is the collection of microorganisms, such as bacteria and fungi, that exist in the gut. People with schizophrenia often have dysbiosis, an imbalance in the gut microbiome. Researchers are intrigued by and are exploring this association.

In addition, experts are considering how diet might contribute to psychotic disorder. Researchers, for example, are looking into the use of omega-3 fatty acids to add to the treatment of psychotic disorders. The role of B9 (folate) is also being studied.

The importance of balanced diets, particularly for pregnant women, is stressed in the research literature. Malnutrition is linked to higher rates of schizophrenia. During World War II (1939–1945), the Nazi regime rationed food in the Netherlands. Women who were pregnant during that time gave birth to children who had higher rates of schizophrenia diagnoses later in life.

CHAPTER
TWO

HOW ARE PSYCHOTIC DISORDERS DIAGNOSED?

No specific medical tests, such as blood tests or X-rays, yet exist that can diagnose psychotic disorders. Instead, a knowledgeable professional spends time listening to and observing the person with psychosis, reviewing medical records, and even talking to family members. He or she diagnoses a particular psychotic disorder by looking for a designated group of symptoms. This professional might be a primary care physician, nurse practitioner, or social worker, but is often a psychologist or psychiatrist. A group of these professionals may collaborate on a diagnosis.

Most mental health professionals rely on the *DSM-5* to diagnose psychotic disorders. Each disorder has a group of symptoms that must be met for the diagnosis to be made. The first step in diagnosis is to administer medical tests to determine if disease, prescribed medication,

A medical professional, such as a psychiatrist, talks to and observes a patient as part of the diagnosis process. The psychiatrist will also review medical records and talk to people who know the patient.

or street drug or alcohol use might be responsible for the psychosis. These tests might include blood and urine samples, an MRI scan to study images of the brain, or an electroencephalogram (EEG) to measure electrical activity in the brain. It is important to diagnose these other possible causes of psychosis early because the treatments might be different, and it is vital to begin the proper treatment quickly.

DIAGNOSING SCHIZOPHRENIA

With these medical tests completed, the diagnostician can turn her attention to the *DSM-5* and consider the list of psychotic disorders and associated symptoms found there. Among the listed disorders is schizophrenia. The characteristic symptoms of schizophrenia are delusions, hallucinations, disorganized speech, grossly disorganized behavior or catatonia, and negative symptoms. According to the *DSM-5*, an individual with schizophrenia must have at least two of the characteristic symptoms for at least one month, and at least one of them must be delusion, hallucination, or disorganized speech. Some symptoms must be present for at least six months. Delusions, hallucinations, disorganized speech, and grossly disorganized behavior are known as positive symptoms. This means that these symptoms are excessive versions or distortions of what would be seen in a healthy individual, rather than the absence of a normal behavior.

DEFINING DELUSIONS

Delusions are false beliefs that a person holds even when he or she is presented with evidence that contradicts the belief or proves it to be untrue or illogical. For example, a person with delusions might believe that he is the president of the United States. Even when shown current newspapers that demonstrate that someone else is the president, the person will remain convinced that he holds the office. Another individual with delusions might think that aliens are communicating with her through the television, and no logical argument can shake her of that belief.

The diagnostician must consider delusions in a cultural context, however. In certain cultures, the person's delusions might be logical or align with the cultural belief system. For example, a person who works with the Central Intelligence Agency (CIA) could logically worry that her phone is being tapped or that people are following her. Because of the culture of her job, those concerns could be completely realistic. As another example, if a person insists that she has been cursed, the diagnostician must consider whether the idea of curses is an accepted part of her culture's religious beliefs.

TYPES OF DELUSIONS

Many varieties of delusions have been observed and categorized. In grandiose delusions, the individual believes herself to be especially powerful or talented. She might think she is a famous historical figure or claim to have created an elixir that offers eternal life. A persecutory delusion is one in which the person thinks that others are ridiculing him, spying on him, following him, or attempting to do him harm.

Grandiose and persecutory delusions are commonly seen in schizophrenia, as are delusions with themes that involve thoughts. With thought control delusions, a person thinks that outside forces

THE TRUMAN SHOW DELUSION

In her article "A New Kind of Delusion?" Tori DeAngelis discusses a type of delusion defined by Joel Gold, a psychiatrist at New York University School of Medicine, and Ian Gold, a philosopher at McGill University. They call it the Truman Show delusion. In 2002, Joel Gold began to see patients who were describing their delusions and specifically referencing the 1998 movie *The Truman Show*. In the movie, the main character, Truman Burbank, unknowingly is the star of a reality show. All the people in his life, from his family members to his co-workers to the local shopkeepers, are merely actors. The patients coming to Joel Gold believed that they were starring in their own television show and that all those around them were actors.

David Downing, a psychology professor at the University of Indianapolis, says that having cultural allusions in delusions is nothing new. He points out that cultural events of the past, such as World War II (1939–1945) and the Cold War, often fueled the delusions of patients who believed the Germans or Russians were spying on them. It is no surprise, then, that *The Truman Show* finds its way into the delusions of patients.

Joel Gold and Ian Gold believe that the Truman Show delusion is different from previously identified delusions because of its broader scope. In certain other delusions, for instance, only the loved ones are replaced. In the Truman Show delusion, everyone in the patient's life is playing a role.

29

People with delusions might think that others are conspiring against them. This may make them unreasonably suspicious of the people they meet in everyday life.

are controlling her thoughts. There are thought insertions or thought withdrawal delusions, in which the individual believes that someone or some group is placing thoughts into her brain or plucking them out. When an individual has thought broadcasting delusions, she thinks that her thoughts are being shared aloud and that everyone can hear them. In mind reading delusions, she believes that others can privately know her thoughts.

Delusions of reference occur when a person thinks that ordinary objects, comments, and events are meant for or directed at him.

In her book *A Beautiful Mind: The Life of Mathematical Genius and Nobel Laureate John Nash*, Sylvia Nasar recounts the story of Nash, a mathematician who won the Nobel Prize in Economic Sciences. Nash had his first psychotic episode when he was thirty years old and was diagnosed with paranoid schizophrenia. Nash had delusions of reference. While teaching at the Massachusetts Institute of Technology (MIT), he recalled, "I got the impression that other people at MIT were wearing red neckties so I would notice them."[7] In 1959, also at MIT, Nash insisted that an article in the *New York Times* was a message from another galaxy that only he could decode. This is another example of a reference delusion because the message was supposedly sent for him.

THE ILL BRAIN PARADOX

In a conversation between Nash and Harvard professor George Mackey, Nash clarifies one of the central paradoxes of psychotic disorders: the person's delusions and hallucinations are coming from his trusted, but dysfunctional, brain. Mackey could not fathom how Nash had believed that aliens were communicating with him. "'Because,' Nash said slowly in his soft reasonable Southern drawl, as if talking to himself, 'the ideas I had about supernatural beings came to me the same way my mathematical ideas did. So I took them seriously.'"[8]

In his book *Surviving Schizophrenia*, Torrey also writes about this key difficulty that people with schizophrenia face: "You must use your malfunctioning brain to assess the malfunction of your brain."[9] This challenge that Nash and Torrey articulate so well is likely a reason that about 50 percent of those with schizophrenia do not have insight about their own illness; they refuse to accept that they are ill. This lack of insight is known as anosognosia.

RARE DELUSIONS: CAPGRAS AND COTARD

Esmé Weijun Wang, author of *The Collected Schizophrenias: Essays*, has been diagnosed with schizoaffective disorder. In her book, she discusses the two rare types of delusions that she has: Capgras and Cotard. With Capgras delusion, she believes that her loved ones have been replaced by doubles. She writes that there are times when she is certain that her husband has been replaced by an identical robot. With Cotard delusion, Wang is convinced that she is dead. At one point, the delusion led her to think she was in an afterlife and had been given the chance to live a kinder existence than she had previously. But at another time, the delusion took a darker turn, and she believed she was destined to exist in a type of hell. She writes, "In this scenario, I was doomed to wander forever in a world that was not mine, in a body that was not mine; I was doomed to be surrounded by creatures and so-called people who mimicked the lovely world that I'd once known, but were now fictions and could evoke no emotion in me."[10]

Wang cites the work of Hans Debruyne and coauthors, who suggest that Capgras and Cotard delusions are related to one another. Both types of delusion cause difficulties in the same locations in the brain. She writes that both delusions affect the fusiform face area and the amygdala, which is responsible for processing emotions. Therefore, when the individual with these delusions looks at loved ones and does not feel the appropriate emotions, she concludes that her loved ones must be replacements.

During her Cotard delusions, Wang's lack of emotional connection to others led her to believe that she must be dead.

WHAT ARE HALLUCINATIONS?

Hallucinations, another symptom of schizophrenia, occur when a person perceives something with one of her five senses in the absence of external stimuli. In other words, she sees, hears, feels, smells, or tastes something that does not exist. For instance, she might see trolls or feel worms crawling under her skin. An individual with schizophrenia often has auditory hallucinations, which are commonly a voice or multiple voices commenting on or ridiculing the person with schizophrenia. Auditory hallucinations are the most common type. If sensory hallucinations other than auditory are most prevalent, it suggests medication or drug-induced psychosis, or it may imply that another underlying medical condition might be the cause.

With hallucinations, as with delusions, the person's culture must be considered during diagnosis. For example, some religions believe in visual manifestations of saints or deities. In people of those religions, having this type of hallucination might be culturally explainable.

In his article "Psychosis," David B. Arciniegas explains that hallucinations are "evidence of impaired reality when the individual experiencing them is unable to recognize the hallucinatory nature of such experiences."[11] In other words, the person having the hallucination is convinced it is real, and this lack of insight is key to diagnosing the hallucination as a psychotic symptom.

Arciniegas mentions that healthy people sometimes experience hallucinations that are not evidence of psychosis, such as the visual

Hallucinations can be a frightening experience. They are not exclusive to psychotic disorders, but they are one of several typical symptoms.

hallucinations that accompany migraines. It is not unusual to have dreamlike hallucinations upon waking, known as hypnopompic hallucinations, or while falling asleep, referred to as hypnagogic hallucinations. And it is not uncommon to hear someone calling your own name. Such phenomena can exist outside of psychosis.

OTHER SYMPTOMS

The next symptom of schizophrenia is disordered speech. A person with schizophrenia often has difficulty constructing meaningful sentences or conversing in a coherent way. He might put words together that have little or no connection. This phenomenon is called word salad. The individual might add unrelated details that veer away from the focus of conversation and never return, which is called tangentiality. Circumstantiality, on the other hand, occurs when the conversation wanders far from the point but eventually returns. Sometimes, the person even makes up nonsense words, or neologisms, in the midst of speaking. He might repeat words, or he might stop talking mid-sentence as if the words were plucked from his mind, which is called thought blocking.

Grossly disorganized or catatonic behavior is another characteristic of schizophrenia. With grossly disorganized behavior, a person might act oddly. She could appear disheveled or be dressed inappropriately for the weather. On the other hand, the behavior might be catatonic. Someone with catatonic behavior might not move or speak at all. The person could repeat another's words, echolalia, or repeat another's actions, echopraxia. Other elements of catatonic behavior include repetitive movements, awkward postures, and unexplained agitation.

Negative symptoms are another symptom of schizophrenia listed in the *DSM-5*. Negative symptoms are abilities that are lacking or diminished compared to healthy people. Michelle Quilter, the director of dialectical behavior therapy (DBT) at Lifeskills South Florida, explains, "The negative symptoms of schizophrenia are similar to the symptoms of major depressive disorder, and could even be confused when making a differential diagnosis."[12] A person with schizophrenia might not be able to show emotion on her face or reflect emotion in her voice. This is called having a flat affect. Avolition is often seen in schizophrenia. It means that the person cannot initiate or perform tasks. The person might also have anhedonia, the inability to find happiness in things that once brought her pleasure. According to the *DSM-5*, a person's functioning at work, at school, in interpersonal relationships, or with self-care must be much lower than it was before the illness for the person to be diagnosed.

Schizophrenia can also affect an individual's cognitive abilities. People with schizophrenia can have poor executive functioning. That is, they have trouble processing information and making decisions. They can have problems with attention. They may have difficulty storing new memories to use on immediate tasks. These symptoms can make daily life a significant challenge.

In his book, Torrey reflects on a cognitive deficit that can be found in schizophrenia. He writes that people with schizophrenia might not think abstractly. Instead, their thinking is often concrete in nature. When asked to explain the phrase, "People in glass houses shouldn't throw stones," a person with schizophrenia might respond, "Because glass will cut you." They may miss the phrase's abstract meaning that because no one is without faults, you should not judge others.

SCHIZOPHRENIFORM DISORDER AND BRIEF PSYCHOTIC DISORDER

To be diagnosed, schizophreniform disorder requires the same characteristic symptoms as schizophrenia, but the time frame differs. For schizophreniform disorder, the required symptoms must be evident for at least one month, but less than six months. A diagnosis of a brief psychotic episode also includes the same symptomatology as schizophrenia without the negative symptoms. As the category suggests, this is an illness of short duration, of at least one day but less than one month.

These shorter duration psychotic disorders have a prevalence rate of one or two in 100,000 people. They affect approximately twice as many women as men. The age of onset is a bit older than with schizophrenia, and the outcomes are generally better.

SCHIZOAFFECTIVE DISORDER

Schizoaffective disorder has the characteristic symptoms of schizophrenia with an added mood episode—either a major depressive episode or a manic episode—as a component. A person who is diagnosed with schizoaffective disorder and is experiencing a concurrent depressive episode might feel very sad and hopeless and might even be considering suicide. She might have a change in appetite, eating more or less, and a change in sleep patterns, sleeping longer or experiencing sleep disruptions. She could have little energy and a lack of concentration.

On the other hand, an individual having a concurrent manic episode will likely feel elated and energized. He would not sleep much. He might have racing thoughts. Often, pressured speech is present. Quilter explains that pressured speech "is when the person talks without stopping or listening. It is like the person is trying to get his racing thoughts expressed. Pressured speech can cause anxiety in the listener."[13] A person experiencing a manic episode is likely to act impulsively. There might be excessive shopping, gambling, or risky, uncharacteristic sexual encounters.

The challenging part of diagnosing schizoaffective disorder is that mood disorders, such as major depressive disorder and bipolar disorder, can have a psychotic component. How can a mental health professional diagnose schizoaffective disorder accurately? Quilter says, "If mood stabilizing medication is given to the patient and there is no psychosis, then major depressive disorder or bipolar disorder is diagnosed. On the other hand, if the psychosis remains in the absence of mood symptoms, then schizoaffective disorder is diagnosed."[14] In other words, mood stabilizing medication should resolve the psychosis of a mood disorder, but it will not do this in a psychotic disorder. Quilter adds that the doctor can also ask the patient's family if he has ever had psychosis during a stable mood to make the differential diagnosis.

Wang was diagnosed with schizoaffective disorder, bipolar type, and she had Capgras and Cotard delusions. She also experienced auditory hallucinations. She writes, "Showering became a challenge shortly after I began to hallucinate in college; my first experience with hearing voices occurred when a phantasm in the dorm showers intoned, 'I hate you.'"[15]

In addition, she had visual hallucinations in the form of shadowy demons coming at her.

"Showering became a challenge shortly after I began to hallucinate in college; my first experience with hearing voices occurred when a phantasm in the dorm showers intoned, 'I hate you.'"[15]

– Esmé Weijun Wang, who was diagnosed with schizoaffective disorder, on her hallucinations

Wang also describes the mood portions of her disorder. Before her spring break at Yale University, she experienced a manic episode: "My thoughts skittered through like messages on ticker tape, and I wanted to run instead of walk; I punched a tree on Cross Campus, shuddering with an energy my body couldn't contain."[16]

Soon after, a depressive episode hit, and she had suicidal thoughts. At this time, she sought help and was hospitalized.

DELUSIONAL DISORDER

Delusional disorder requires a person to have one delusion or more for at least a month, and it also requires that the characteristic symptoms for schizophrenia have not been met. For the most part, the disorder is without hallucinations, unless the hallucinations are of the same theme as the delusion and are not the prominent feature. The types of delusions found in delusional disorder might be grandiose or persecutory. The delusions might be erotomanic, in which the person is convinced that someone, often a famous person, is in love with her. Jealous delusions occur when the person believes that her significant other is being unfaithful. Somatic delusion is one that involves body functions or sensations. For instance, a person with this type of delusion may be convinced that she is dying of cancer. Delusional disorder occurs in approximately 0.2 percent of people, making it rarer than schizophrenia. It is slightly more prevalent in females than males, and the age of onset is a bit older than with schizophrenia.

PSYCHOTIC DISORDER DUE TO ANOTHER MEDICAL DISORDER

There is a category in the *DSM-5* for diagnosing psychotic disorder due to another medical disorder. This is because many other medical conditions can cause psychosis. Conditions such as brain tumor, stroke, Alzheimer's disease, Lewy body dementia, Parkinson's disease, and epilepsy can have psychosis as a symptom. The symptoms present for this diagnosis must be hallucination or delusion or both.

In the article "When the Body Attacks the Mind," Moises Velasquez-Manoff writes about another medical disorder that mimics the psychosis of mental illness. Thirteen-year-old Sasha Egger thought that people were coming to hurt his family. In a short while, he forgot how to play his favorite card game and was walking around aimlessly. When he was hospitalized, one of the specialists diagnosed him with a mental illness and administered antipsychotics, which did him no good.

Fortunately, his mother was a child psychiatrist, and she approached a neurologist colleague for help. The neurologist diagnosed Sasha with autoimmune encephalitis, which inflames the brain. Sasha's own immune system had attacked the receptors in his brain, causing his psychotic symptoms. He was given medication to suppress his immune response, and he recovered immediately. Unfortunately, Sasha has had several relapses since then. Sasha's mother told Velasquez-Manoff, "Psychosis is like a fever. It's a symptom of a lot of different illnesses."[17]

OTHER DIAGNOSES

The *DSM-5* also has a category for substance/medication-induced psychotic disorder. Prescribed medication, including opioids and barbiturates, can sometimes cause psychosis. Many street drugs are known to result in psychosis as well. Quilter says that the professionals at Lifeskills South Florida have seen a large increase in marijuana-induced psychosis. Researchers suggest that the increase in tetrahydrocannabinol (THC) in marijuana may be to blame. Amphetamines; classic hallucinogens, such as lysergic acid diethylamide (LSD) and psilocybin, also known as magic mushrooms; phencyclidine (PCP), and other substances can also cause psychosis. The psychosis can subside after the drugs leave the body, but in some cases the psychosis lasts for a

In addition to being dangerous for many other reasons, street drugs can cause psychosis. Drug-induced psychosis has its own category in the _DSM_.

longer time. In order to diagnose this psychotic disorder, delusions or hallucinations or both must be noted, and other medical conditions must be ruled out.

The _DSM-5_ allows mental health professionals to use the category _specified schizophrenic spectrum and other psychotic disorder_ if they have a specific reason why the disorder does not fit the symptoms of the other psychotic disorders. The _unspecified schizophrenic spectrum and other psychotic disorder_ category can be used if the symptoms do not match any other psychotic disorder and the mental health professional does not wish to specify a diagnosis. Perhaps the patient had taken an illicit substance, but the professional suspects that schizoaffective disorder may be underlying. She might use this category while referring the patient to another professional to make a more definitive diagnosis.

CHAPTER
THREE

WHAT IS LIFE LIKE WITH PSYCHOTIC DISORDERS?

Living with a psychotic disorder can be challenging. It requires strength and persistence on the part of the person with the disorder. It also requires strength, understanding, and compassion on the part of family members and friends. Many times, the support of family and close friends plays an important part. Another key is a partnership between the individual and knowledgeable mental health professionals.

THE PRODROME

An individual who suffers from schizophrenia and related psychotic disorders will rarely experience psychotic episodes unexpectedly. In general, the individual will experience early, gradual, non-specific changes. This is known as the prodromal phase. It consists of early symptoms that can make an appearance from weeks to years before an acute psychotic episode. The earlier a psychotic disorder is diagnosed, the more effective

Withdrawing from socializing with others can be one of the early gradual changes that happens before an acute psychotic episode. Watching for such prodromal symptoms can help medical professionals make a diagnosis quickly.

the treatment and the better the chance of recovery. Identifying prodromal symptoms can be useful for early diagnosis.

The prodromal symptoms include unusual suspiciousness, changes in perceptions, and withdrawal from social interaction. The person might have trouble thinking clearly or concentrating. Her grades at school might drop or work performance might decline. She could lack energy or initiative, so she might be late to school or work—or not go at all.

Difficulty with speech can be a prodromal symptom. In their article "Understanding the Schizophrenia Prodrome," Manju George and

43

INVOLUNTARY HOSPITALIZATION

Psychiatric hospitals are sometimes necessary for a person who is experiencing an acute psychotic episode. Families can try to convince their adult loved ones to enter a hospital voluntarily. However, the anosognosia can prove a barrier because the individual does not believe she needs treatment. This is where the debate over involuntary hospitalization and forced medication begins.

Most US states allow for involuntary commitment of an individual with mental illness if he is a danger to himself or a danger to others. The conditions for involuntary commitment are very specific to protect the person's civil rights. Some advocates, such as Torrey, believe in the necessity of involuntary commitment and forced medication for those with schizophrenia and related disorders. His argument is based on his belief that a person with a brain disease cannot always be relied upon to make a measured decision about the need for either hospitalization or medication. He writes, "The right to be free of the symptoms of a brain disease must be weighed against the individual's right to privacy."[1]

On the other side of the argument are individuals with psychotic disorders who have been involuntarily hospitalized. For instance, Wang writes that she was involuntarily hospitalized three times with schizoaffective disorder, and it horrified her. She writes, "I maintain, years later, that not one of my three involuntary hospitalizations helped me. I believe that being held in a psychiatric ward against my will remains among the most scarring of my traumas."[2]

1. E. Fuller Torrey, Surviving Schizophrenia: A Family Manual, Sixth Edition. New York: Harper Perennial, 2013, p. 268.

2. Esmé Weijun Wang, The Collected Schizophrenias: Essays. Minneapolis, MN: Graywolf Press, 2019, p. 110.

coauthors write that prodromal speech might include "digressive, vague, overelaborate or circumstantial speech, or poverty of speech, or poverty of content of speech."[18] In other words, the person might talk a lot without making a point, or the person might barely speak at all.

The individual with prodromal symptoms can experience disruptions in eating and sleeping. Personal hygiene can be lacking. For example, the person might not shower for weeks or stop brushing his teeth. The prodromal symptoms can also be less specific. They might include a general feeling of anxiety, depression, or irritability. Quasi-psychotic experiences, such as magical thinking or feelings of paranoia, can also be in the mix. For example, the person might display a sudden interest in out-of-body experiences or the meaning of numbers.

IDENTIFYING THE PRODROME

Prodromal symptoms can be tricky to identify because they can mirror normal behavior. For example, some adolescents withdraw from their families and spend a lot of time in their bedrooms. They might not wash their clothes as often as they need. In addition, some of the same symptoms can also indicate other mental illnesses. For instance, a person with sleeping and eating problems can be experiencing depression or mania. If a group of prodromal symptoms is observed, a mental health professional can make an informed diagnosis.

The prodrome before the first psychotic episode is called the initial prodrome. The prodrome that comes before subsequent psychoses is known as the relapse prodrome. Not surprisingly, the initial prodrome is more difficult to identify because it has not yet been experienced by the person with psychotic disorder and has not been seen by her family or friends.

With relapse prodrome, on the other hand, the person with psychosis can sometimes identify the early symptoms specific to his own disorder. A barrier to this is that a large number of those with psychotic disorder have anosognosia and do not believe that they are ill. In situations like these, family members and close friends can help note the relapse prodrome and try to convince the person with psychotic disorder to seek help. Then, perhaps her mental health professional can adjust her medication and avoid acute psychosis and hospitalization.

A woman who goes by the pseudonym Lily Fox was only six years old when her mother had her first psychotic episode. Now, more than thirty years later, she and her mom can identify the relapse prodromal symptoms. They begin with generalized anxiety. Fox's mother says she feels like she is "jumping out of her skin."[19] Then, telephone numbers seem to be messages to her. Fox's mother begins to speak of a big secret. As soon as these symptoms appear, they contact her psychiatrist, who adjusts the dose or type of medication.

In her book *The Center Cannot Hold*, Elyn R. Saks discusses the relapse prodromal symptoms of her schizophrenia. Her speech becomes disorganized in a nonsensical, wordplay manner. Saks recalls what she said, including things such as, "I'm just kidding around. Kidding has to do with sheep."[20] Saks would also begin to talk about killing people with her thoughts. One of her friends, who recognized the early symptoms, placed a call to Saks's psychiatrist. He increased the dosage of her antipsychotic medicine, and hospitalization was averted. About her friends' support at this time, Saks writes, "They were calm, they did the right thing, and the moment passed."[21]

> "They were calm, they did the right thing, and the moment passed."[21]
>
> *– Elyn R. Saks, who was diagnosed with schizophrenia, on her friends' support during severe symptoms*

THE HUMAN TOLL OF PSYCHOTIC DISORDER

Psychotic disorders can take a terrible toll on an individual. The person can experience psychotic episodes that include delusions and hallucinations. These symptoms are often frightening and confusing. Fox's mother had paranoid delusions that people were talking about her and that everyone around her had a secret that they were not sharing with her.

She was also convinced that her husband was having an affair. These delusions were not only scary, but also left her feeling alone because she believed that those closest to her were plotting against her. In addition, Fox's mom had auditory hallucinations that frightened her. She heard voices from the television set that were talking directly to her.

Saks's delusion that she was killing people with her thoughts and that others were trying to murder her were terrifying. She hallucinated demons that were ready to take her life: "The room was full of swirling, taunting demons, forces coming through the walls and ceiling."[22] She writes of a visit to her psychiatrist's office during one of her horror-filled psychotic periods: "I headed straight for the corner, crouched down on the floor, and began to shake."[23]

In addition to the sheer terror of the psychosis, psychotic disorders can interfere with the person's promising future and goals. Fox's mother had to stop working until she recovered. But most devastating to her was her inability to adequately care for her children. The children had to spend time with extended family while her health improved. To this day, she feels guilty about not being available to nurture her children.

Wang was a promising student at Yale University. She was hospitalized twice for her schizoaffective disorder while attending Yale. In between hospitalizations, she studied conscientiously. She also continued to suffer with her mental illness. She writes, "I lay writhing on the floor, sobbing, caught in knotty torment."[24] Even though she was progressing through the academic program, the university insisted that she leave due to her hospitalizations. She writes, "Yale told me to leave immediately. I was not allowed to reenter campus and so someone confiscated my student ID."[25] In this abrupt and harsh manner, Wang's academic career was derailed.

STIGMA

Individuals with psychotic disorder deal not only with challenging symptoms but also the stigma of having a mental illness. Stigma means that many people in society think about and treat people with a psychotic disorder differently. Often this is because those people are not educated about psychotic disorders. Because they misunderstand mental illness, others can be afraid of and avoid those with psychotic disorder.

As Catherine Giasson, MSN, RN, eloquently writes about the stigma of schizophrenia, "Sadly while it is the illness that causes the stigma, it is the *person* who is stigmatized. With no understanding of the illness, many people are afraid of a person who has schizophrenia. The portrayal of the illness on television and in the news media supports this fear and increases stigma."[26] When the media portrays individuals with schizophrenia or related disorders, they are often acting violently. However, this is not an accurate depiction. Studies indicate that people with schizophrenia are no more violent than the general population. The abuse of substances does increase violent behavior, however.

> "Sadly while it is the illness that causes the stigma, it is the *person* who is stigmatized. With no understanding of the illness, many people are afraid of a person who has schizophrenia. The portrayal of the illness on television and in the news media supports this fear and increases stigma."[26]
>
> – Catherine Giasson, MSN, RN, on the stigma of schizophrenia

Stigma can leave the person with a psychotic disorder feeling isolated. Practically speaking, she might encounter discrimination when seeking a job or a place to live. She may even lose a chance to attend a prestigious university, as Wang did. Because they know these concrete outcomes of societal stigma, people with psychotic disorder may hide their diagnosis. Most importantly, stigma can keep people with psychotic disorders from seeking the needed treatment.

The stigma concerning mental illness originated, in part, from the teaching of the French philosopher René Descartes, who lived in the 1600s. Descartes theorized that the body and mind were separate, and this dualistic idea is still widespread. Many people view mental illness as distinct from bodily or physical illness, when in reality the mind is just part of the body. And those people may be more understanding and accepting when it comes to a person with a physical illness.

But research into psychotic disorders, such as schizophrenia, is indeed discovering that these mental illnesses actually are also physical in nature. Torrey explains, "Schizophrenia is firmly and unequivocally established to be a brain disease, just as surely as multiple sclerosis, Parkinson's disease and Alzheimer's disease are established as brain diseases."[27] In his book *A Brother Finds Answers in Biological Science*, biologist Ronald Chase predicts a time when the physical element of mental disorders will be better recognized. He writes, "The term *mental illness* will eventually be abandoned in favor of an alternative term that recognizes the physical basis of behavioral and psychological disorders."[28]

Societal stigma about psychotic disorder is so pervasive that Fox's immediate

> "The term *mental illness* will eventually be abandoned in favor of an alternative term that recognizes the physical basis of behavioral and psychological disorders."[28]
>
> – Biologist Ronald Chase

family never discussed her mother's illness in detail. The shame of the disorder was such that Fox did not even share her mother's diagnosis with friends. Therefore, the stigma stopped family members from communicating with one another and isolated them from outside relationships. Fox's extended family was not educated about psychotic disorder and demonstrated little compassion for Fox's mother. They couldn't understand why her mother didn't just pull herself together. They saw the psychotic disorder as a personal weakness and a way for her mother to escape responsibilities. Would family members have said the same if Fox's mother had cancer? Likely not. This was stigma at work.

SELF-CARE

Since antipsychotic medication is generally effective for reducing psychotic symptoms, it is key for a person with psychotic disorder to stay on their proper dose of medication. A pill container with a compartment for each day of the week might help the individual remember to take the medication daily. With many medications, there is an option to use a long-acting injectable medication for those who don't want to take medication every day.

People with psychotic disorder stop taking their medication for various reasons. Anosognosia, the lack of recognition that they are ill, keeps them from seeing the need for the medication, so they don't take it. Other people begin to feel better and wean themselves from the medication. Some are bothered by the side effects. In some cases, paranoid delusions can lead an individual to believe that the medication has been poisoned.

It is important that the person diagnosed with psychotic disorder take the best care of herself possible. This may seem simple for those without a mental health issue, but for someone struggling with a serious disorder,

Something as simple as eating healthful food can help people with psychotic disorders feel better. Limiting stress and getting good sleep are other steps they can take.

taking care of himself can be a significant challenge. The National Alliance on Mental Illness (NAMI) suggests limiting stress, which can trigger psychosis, while at work or school. Exercising is a solid way to manage stress and regulate mood. Getting a good amount of sleep and eating nutritiously can also help with staying healthy.

NAMI also advises avoiding alcohol and drugs because they can interfere with antipsychotic medication. Alcohol and drug use are frequently a problem among those with psychotic disorders. If substance use disorder is present, it should be treated. Finally, NAMI recommends staying socially active. A peer support group might be a good option for maintaining social interactions.

SUPPORTIVE FAMILIES

Family support is generally crucial in keeping a person with psychotic disorder well. The family might be the first to identify the prodromal symptoms and encourage the individual to seek help. Family members can also remind the individual to take his antipsychotic medication regularly. NAMI recommends that the family remain positive and not be critical. They can aid the person in setting realistic life goals.

Experts advise not arguing with the individual about her delusions or hallucinations. It will not do any good and will likely upset everyone involved. But do not play along, either. Instead, stay calm and acknowledge their perceptions. For example, Fox would tell her mother, "I understand that is what you are feeling. It is your illness and medication will make you better."[29]

Having a person with psychotic disorder in the family presents myriad challenges. The recovery process and possibility of relapses can cause stress and emotional upheaval in the family. For Fox, as for many blood relatives of someone with psychotic disorder, there is the fear of inheriting the illness.

Also, the family dynamics change. The person with psychotic disorder needs care and often becomes the focus of the family. In Fox's case, her mother was at the center of her father's attention, which left little parental nurturing for the children. In addition, because her mother was unable to care for her younger sibling, Fox took on parenting duties when she herself was still a child. She recalls a time when her mother was ill. Fox placed her sister in the basement and left loud music playing to drown out her mother's yelling. Fox was playing the role of protector. The family can suffer economically as well. In Fox's situation, the family's income dropped when her mother was hospitalized and during her recovery because her mother couldn't work. And, of course, psychiatric hospitals, medications, and therapy can be costly.

POSTPARTUM PSYCHOSIS

Postpartum psychosis is psychosis that occurs soon after a woman gives birth, usually within the first two weeks. Postpartum psychosis is rare; only 1 in 1,000 women are diagnosed with it. However, the rate is much higher for women with existing mental health disorders. Changes in hormones, a lack of sleep after birth, and birth complications may be contributing factors to the illness.

In her book *When Postpartum Packs a Punch: Fighting Back and Finding Joy*, Kristina Cowan recounts the experiences of Teresa Twomey, who had postpartum psychosis after the birth of her first child. Her psychosis involved delusions, hallucinations, and cognitive symptoms. She had paranoid delusions that her husband was planning to leave her. Twomey also had auditory hallucinations. At times, when her husband was at work, she heard someone enter her home and riffle through paperwork. She also believed she heard people whispering and plotting against her. She had thoughts of throwing her infant down the stairs and one visual hallucination of her harming the baby. Cognitively, Twomey had trouble concentrating while reading or watching television.

The outcome of postpartum psychosis is usually positive. This type of psychosis is normally brief and leaves no lasting effects. The treatment can be antipsychotic medications and medications to address any mood component. Between 72 and 88 percent of postpartum psychosis cases have a mood element.

Even though the long-term prognosis for postpartum psychosis is good, it is vital for both the health of the mother and infant that a diagnosis is made quickly and treatment begins right away. Suicide and infanticide occur in a small percentage of cases. One such tragic situation took place in 2001 in Texas when Andrea Yates, who had postpartum psychosis, drowned her five children in a bathtub.

Supportive families can make a big difference for people with psychotic disorders. Family members can observe symptoms, remind their loved one to take medication, and help set life goals.

Ron Powers and his wife faithfully supported their sons Kevin and Dean, who were diagnosed with schizoaffective disorder and schizophrenia, respectively. Tragically, Kevin died by suicide in his early twenties. Approximately 5–6 percent of those with schizophrenia die by suicide. Powers insists that no matter the family challenges of caring for an individual with psychotic disorder, early and persistent family support is necessary. He writes, "When symptoms occur in a loved one, assume the worst until a professional convinces you otherwise. Act quickly and keep acting. If necessary, act to the limit of your means. Tough advice. Tough world."[30]

Torrey offers a solid tip for finding just such a competent mental health professional to diagnose and treat those with psychotic disorder. He suggests asking medical personnel to whom they would send a loved one for care. This information from those in the know can prove valuable.

THE EFFECTS OF DEINSTITUTIONALIZATION

Some of the difficulties that those with psychotic disorders face in the United States can be traced back to deinstitutionalization. In the mid-1950s, the first antipsychotic medication, chlorpromazine, was introduced in the United States. It was effective in reducing the positive symptoms of psychotic disorders. The effectiveness of chlorpromazine, coupled with the uncovering of the crowded and deplorable conditions of state psychiatric hospitals, led to the closure of many of these facilities and the release of 560,000 patients. The plan was that these patients would be better served in psychiatric clinics in their own communities.

Sadly, the government funding for building and staffing these clinics ran dry, and psychiatric patients were left without necessary treatments in many cases. Fewer than 650 community centers were constructed—less than half the hoped-for number. Many people with psychotic disorder are now unable to find appropriate treatment in their communities.

Those without treatment can become homeless. In turn, their behavior in active psychosis can result in their being arrested. In this way, prisons have become the modern psychiatric facilities, but they are grossly inadequate to provide care to psychotic individuals. Citing a 2015 statistic, Powers writes, "The mentally ill account for more than 350,000 inmates in U.S. prisons, more than ten times those in psychiatric hospitals."[31] People with psychotic symptoms make up significant percentages of those inmates.

CHAPTER
FOUR

HOW ARE PSYCHOTIC DISORDERS TREATED?

I n general, health care professionals speak of treatment rather than cure when working with most psychotic disorders. Today's treatments target particular symptoms, such as hallucinations and delusions. These psychotic disorders are considered chronic in nature, just like diseases such as diabetes, and they require consistent symptom management. A few psychotic disorders are not necessarily chronic. For example, brief psychotic disorder can be a one-time event connected to a stressful life incident. Substance-induced psychotic disorders may subside when the substance, such as an illicit drug, is no longer being used. In addition, a psychotic disorder due to another medical condition might be cured if the underlying medical condition can be addressed. When discussing schizophrenia, Lynn DeLisi explains this concept of treatment rather than cure: "Medications do not yet 'cure' the actual biological basis for the illness, but are likely to be effective for suppressing the symptoms much like aspirin suppresses the fever and headache from influenza without actually resolving the infection."[32]

One early therapy was called electroconvulsive therapy (ECT). It was first used by Italian psychiatrist Ugo Cerletti in 1938. He applied electricity to the brains of patients to induce convulsions. Cerletti recorded some success with patients who had schizophrenia. The technique gained acceptance in the psychiatric community and was used extensively between 1940 and 1960. A form of ECT is still used today. The modern ECT is administered under general anesthesia. The electrical stimulation can be directed to the nondominant lobe to reduce the side effect of memory loss. Currently, ECT is most effective with those who have medication-resistant depressive disorder. It is seldom used for psychotic disorders, but it can be helpful for those psychotic disorders that are medication-resistant or that have a mood component.

> "Medications do not yet 'cure' the actual biological basis for the illness, but are likely to be effective for suppressing the symptoms much like aspirin suppresses the fever and headache from influenza without actually resolving the infection."[32]
>
> – Psychiatrist Lynn DeLisi on schizophrenia treatment

The current treatments for psychotic disorders include medication, known as antipsychotic medication, and various types of therapy, such as peer group support or cognitive behavioral therapy for psychosis. In addition, there are cutting-edge treatments. They include intelligent real-time therapy, which uses technology to deliver therapeutic intervention, and transcranial magnetic stimulation, which is being studied for relief of psychotic symptoms.

FIRST-GENERATION ANTIPSYCHOTIC MEDICATIONS

In 1950, French chemist Paul Charpentier was working on an antihistamine to combat allergies. The medication he created was called chlorpromazine. Henri Laborit, a French surgeon, recognized the medication's potential to help patients with psychosis. Intrigued by the reported calming effect of the drug, two French psychiatrists, Pierre Deniker and Jean Delay, administered chlorpromazine to their patients with psychosis and noted remarkable effects. The medication relieved positive symptoms—hallucinations, delusions, and some disordered speech—particularly in those with schizophrenia. In 1954, the United States Food and Drug Administration approved the use of chlorpromazine in the United States.

Chlorpromazine was the first of the first-generation antipsychotic (FGA) medications, also known as typical antipsychotics. Other FGAs were soon developed, including haloperidol and fluphenazine. The FGAs proved so effective in suppressing the positive symptoms of psychotic disorders that these patients were able to leave psychiatric hospitals in large numbers. The FGAs, however, are less effective in relieving negative or cognitive symptoms.

Because schizophrenia is the most studied psychotic disorder, much of what is known about how antipsychotic medications work in the brain is through schizophrenic-centered research. Researchers have found that these medications block the dopamine receptors in the brains of individuals with schizophrenia, which suppresses excessive dopamine action in their brains. Five major dopamine receptors have been identified in the brain; they are known as D1 through D5. The FGAs target and block the D2 receptors.

The FGAs can cause side effects such as tremors or stiffness. It is interesting to note that Parkinson's disease, which includes tremors as a symptom, is correlated with a lack of dopamine in the part of the brain responsible for normal movement. Since FGAs lower the action of dopamine in that portion of the brain, it is not surprising to see these types of side effects.

Tardive dyskinesia (TD) may occur with the use of FGAs. TD is characterized by involuntary facial movements, such as grimacing, sucking, or smacking of the lips. It can include jerky or slow movements in other parts of the body as well.

SECOND-GENERATION ANTIPSYCHOTIC MEDICATIONS

Clozapine was introduced in the United States in 1990 and was the start of the second-generation antipsychotic medications (SGAs), also known as the atypical antipsychotic medications. Over time other SGAs, including lurasidone and risperidone, were added. Generally, the SGAs

PEER SUPPORT

The National Alliance on Mental Illness (NAMI) finds peer support beneficial for people with mental illness, including people with psychotic disorder. NAMI offers two peer support groups: Peer-to-Peer, a free eight-session educational program run by trained presenters, and Connection Recovery Support Group, a peer-led group.

These programs allow those with mental health issues, such as psychotic disorders, to interact with others with the same diagnosis. Groups like these help a person with psychotic disorder engage socially and not feel alone. Peer groups offer a safe space to exchange information, such as what type of mental health resources are available in the community or tips on innovative treatments. In a peer support group, people can talk about the day-to-day challenges of living with a psychotic disorder and get practical suggestions for coping with those challenges.

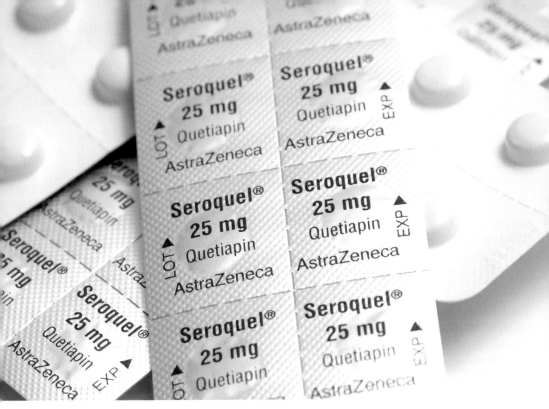

Seroquel is one example of a second-generation antipsychotic medication. It was approved by US medical authorities in 1997.

are as effective as FGAs in the treatment of positive symptoms, and they are less likely to cause the involuntary movement side effects of their predecessors. In his book *The Disordered Mind: What Unusual Brains Tell Us About Ourselves*, Eric R. Kandel writes that SGAs "have a lower affinity for D2 receptors, they block fewer of them, thus leaving movement intact."[33] They also bind to D4 dopamine receptors and serotonin and histamine receptors. However, many of these newer medications can cause metabolic side effects. These metabolic problems can include weight gain and increased risk of high cholesterol and diabetes.

Clozapine has been found to be the most effective treatment for schizophrenia. It has the added benefit of helping rid the individual of suicidal thoughts. But clozapine is often the medication of last resort. This is because it has a rare side effect called agranulocytosis, which is a dangerous drop in white blood cells. A person who is prescribed clozapine must undergo scheduled blood tests to check white blood cell counts. They are checked weekly for the first six months, bi-weekly for the next six months, and monthly after that.

Studies seem to show that the antipsychotic drugs affect different neurotransmitter receptors in the brain. Researchers continue to investigate the exact reasons antipsychotics work. As E. Fuller Torrey plainly states, "The bottom line is that we really don't know how they work. But then, we don't yet know how aspirin works, either."[34]

> "The bottom line is that we really don't know how they work. But then, we don't yet know how aspirin works, either."[34]
>
> – Psychiatrist E. Fuller Torrey on antipsychotics

PRESCRIBING ANTIPSYCHOTICS

It is vital that mental health professionals carefully consider the medication needs of the patient with a psychotic disorder. They must choose a medication that will best address that individual's symptoms. Over time, if the medication is not relieving the symptoms, a different dosage or even another medication can be tried. Due to significant side effects, a key aspect of treatment is to find the lowest possible effective dosage. A new medication can also be prescribed if the side effects are affecting the person's health or are intolerable.

Antipsychotic medications can be prescribed orally, which usually requires them to be taken on a daily basis. On the other hand, some antipsychotics are available as long-lasting injectable medications. Depending on the medication, these injections might be given every few weeks or once a month. Injectable medication may be a good plan for

ANTIPSYCHOTIC
MEDICATIONS

First-Generation Antipsychotic Medications

Generic Name	Brand Name
Chlorpromazine	Thorazine
Fluphenazine	Prolixin
Haloperidol	Haldol
Loxapine	Loxitane
Perphenazine	Trilafon
Thiothixene	Navane
Trifluoperazine	Stelazine

Second-Generation Antipsychotic Medications

Generic Name	Brand Name
Aripiprazole	Abilify
Asenapine	Saphris
Clozapine	Clozaril
Iloperidone	Fanapt
Lurasidone	Latuda
Olanzapine	Zyprexa
Paliperidone	Invega
Quetiapine	Seroquel
Risperidone	Risperdal
Ziprasidone	Geodon

"Schizophrenia Treatment: Medication," National Alliance on Mental Health, n.d. www.nami.org.

people with psychotic disorders who have anosognosia and might not understand their need for antipsychotic medication.

COORDINATED SPECIALTY CARE

The National Institute of Mental Health created a research initiative called Recovery After an Initial Schizophrenia Episode (RAISE). RAISE started in 2008, and its purpose was to study the effectiveness of coordinated specialty care (CSC) when treating individuals who were experiencing their first episode of psychosis.

CSC is a specially designed treatment program. With CSC, a person with first-time psychosis is connected to a team of specialists that work together to offer all types of support to that individual. The team members provide case management, individual and group therapy, work and education support, family education and support, and medication management. One of the keys to CSC is the partnership that is formed between the person with psychosis and the team. The individual takes an active role in decision-making when it comes to her treatment. A psychiatrist or qualified medical professional prescribes medication, deciding the most effective medication, dosage, and method of delivery—oral or injection. The antipsychotic medication is administered in low doses to start. The person participates in individual or group psychotherapy sessions.

A person with psychosis often has trouble going back to school or work. CSC has experts who coordinate the person's return to school or work and coach him in the necessary skills to succeed there. Family support is often vital to people with psychosis. CSC offers education to the person's family so they can understand the disorder and provide support in the most effective ways possible.

The RAISE research project discovered that treatment is more effective if the psychosis is diagnosed quickly. In other words, people with a short duration of untreated psychosis (DUP) did better in treatment than those with a longer DUP. In addition, RAISE found CSC to be a more effective treatment program than typical care programs available in the community. People who received treatment in CSC continued with treatment longer, had more improvement in their symptoms, had better interpersonal relationships, had a better quality of life, and were more involved in work or school than those in typical programs.

COGNITIVE BEHAVIORAL THERAPY FOR PSYCHOSIS

Cognitive behavioral therapy for psychosis (CBTp) can be effective for those with psychotic disorders. Cognitive behavioral therapy addresses the person's present situation and offers practical concrete methods to shift thoughts and behaviors rather than delving deeply into the person's past. Cognitive behavioral therapy focuses on the way that a person's thoughts, behaviors, and feelings are linked. For example, the CBTp therapist might challenge the person with psychosis to change the way she thinks about her hallucinations, which might encourage her to change her behavior and go out with friends, which, in turn, might make her less anxious in social situations.

Sometimes, even with antipsychotic medication, remnants of the positive symptoms remain. CBTp can help patients cope with remaining hallucinations or delusions. In their textbook chapter "Schizophrenia and Other Psychotic Disorders," Nicholas Tarrier and Rumina Taylor examine the research findings for CBTp and conclude: "The evidence for CBTp reducing positive symptoms in chronic, partially remitted patients with schizophrenia is good."[35]

In CBTp, the person with psychosis and the therapist act as a team. They talk together to design coping strategies that work well in the patient's everyday life. For example, a patient might express that her hallucinations or delusions are causing her to feel fearful. The therapist might teach her attention-focusing or relaxation techniques to deal with the hallucinations or delusions. They will practice those techniques over and over again until she feels confident enough to apply them in real-life situations.

> "The evidence for CBTp reducing positive symptoms in chronic, partially remitted patients with schizophrenia is good."[35]
>
> – Authors Nicholas Tarrier and Rumina Taylor

Other coping strategies in CBTp involve internal dialogue, which is what the patient thinks to herself. She can learn to think positive things, such as "I need to sit in this classroom and listen to the teacher. I can do it." These types of encouraging thoughts can foster positive behaviors. The strategy known as reattribution allows the patient to offer herself an alternative explanation for her positive symptoms. For example, she could say, "That seems like a real voice talking to me, but it is only my own thoughts." Tarrier and Taylor explain that once the patient gains some control over the hallucinations or delusions, she can see that they are not all-powerful and can be challenged. In addition, if the person with psychosis feels anxious or upset in certain situations, CBTp can equip her with relaxation methods. She might learn to do some slow deep breathing or quick muscle relaxation exercises.

Delusions can be tightly held and difficult to eliminate. Tarrier and Taylor write that the CBTp therapist can question the logic of the delusion, "pointing out the contradictory evidence in a quizzical or puzzled manner, often known as the 'Columbo technique.'"[36] Columbo was a television detective in the 1970s who always knew who the murderer was but always acted as if he didn't have a clue.

However, this method of challenging delusions is not always successful. Tarrier and Taylor write about a woman who believed that her objectionable thoughts were being broadcast to her fellow church members. She was embarrassed and refused to attend church, which had been an important time of social interaction for her. CBTp taught her to cope with her auditory hallucinations and lessened her anxiety about returning to church. When she went back to church, she was greeted with enthusiasm. Tarrier and Taylor write, "She said that she believed others could hear her thoughts, but because it did not appear to bother them, she was no longer concerned about it either!"[37] Even though the therapy was not able to change her delusional belief, it effectively fostered her return to church and to her social relationships there.

CUTTING-EDGE TECHNOLOGY TREATMENTS

A gap exists in CBTp that technology might fill. The therapist cannot always be with the patient in her everyday life. That is why researchers are examining intelligent real-time therapy to bridge that gap. Technology, such as computers and smartphones, can be utilized so that patients with psychosis can relay their experiences and feelings to their therapist in real time. In addition, interventions that have been planned in the therapist's office can be accessed through these technologies.

In the article "Intelligent Real-Time Therapy: Harnessing the Power of Machine Learning to Optimise the Delivery of Momentary Cognitive-Behavioural Interventions," James Kelly and coauthors write that

During CBTp sessions, therapists can help patients think about their symptoms in a new way. This can help improve the patients' outlook and daily life.

smartphone technology is particularly useful for therapeutic intervention because of its multimedia capabilities. A person can access video, the internet, audio, and more. Kelly writes about one of his patients whose auditory hallucinations were causing him great distress as he went about his daily tasks. The patient "reported using video clips of [comedy duo] Laurel and Hardy to make himself laugh when he was particularly troubled by distressing voices."[38] The authors note that humor can be an effective tool when the patient feels distressed or hopeless.

Technology in the form of computers is also being used in cognitive enhancement therapy. This type of therapy is meant to address the

A smartphone can have many uses in psychotic disorder treatment. It could be used to communicate with a therapist, to watch videos to help cope with symptoms, or even to power virtual reality headsets in cutting-edge therapies.

negative and cognitive symptoms of psychotic disorders that linger even when the individual is taking antipsychotic medication. Shaun Eack and coauthors studied fifty-eight patients with schizophrenia and schizoaffective disorder. The patients underwent cognitive enhancement therapy that involved sixty hours of "computer-assisted neurocognitive training in attention, memory, and problem-solving."[39] In addition, the patients participated in forty-five social-cognitive group therapy sessions, where they worked on interpersonal skills. When tested over the next two years and compared to a group of patients who underwent a different type of personal therapy, the patients who had cognitive enhancement therapy did better in cognition, and particularly in social cognition.

Virtual reality (VR) is being tested for use in the treatment of individuals with psychosis. Patients wear a headset that puts them inside a world generated by a computer. Headphones help complete the illusion. With VR, the person with psychosis can experience real-life situations in a safe, clinical setting. In some VR studies, for example, the patient creates an avatar that represents the voices she hears. She is then able to talk to the avatar, which is controlled by the therapist. The theory is that after these VR experiences, the patient will gain power and control over the auditory hallucinations and feel less distress. VR shows some promise in this regard. VR is also being studied as a method to aid patients with social interaction, cognitive functioning, and vocational training.

Developed in the 1990s, transcranial magnetic stimulation (TMS) is a procedure in which electromagnets are attached to the scalp and magnetic pulses are sent to the brain. Some newer research suggests it may be effective in reducing auditory hallucinations in patients with psychosis, but more studies are needed.

There are reasons for optimism concerning the understanding and treatment of psychotic disorders. Much research continues in order to discover the causes of psychotic disorders, and new treatments are being investigated. And as more people educate themselves about psychotic disorders, the stigma will decrease, making the lives of those with psychotic disorders that much better.

SOURCE NOTES

INTRODUCTION: LOSING TOUCH WITH REALITY

1. "Schizophrenia," *National Institute of Mental Health*, n.d. http://nimh.nih.gov.

CHAPTER 1: WHAT ARE PSYCHOTIC DISORDERS?

2. Quoted in "Thought Disorder," *ScienceDirect*, n.d. www.sciencedirect.com.

3. Quoted in Victor Peralta and Manuel J. Cuesta, "Eugen Bleuler and the Schizophrenias: 100 Years After," *Schizophrenia Bulletin*, vol. 37, no. 6, November 2011, pp. 1118–1120.

4. Nick Craddock, MC O'Donovan, et al., "Psychosis Genetics: Modeling the Relationship Between Schizophrenia, Bipolar Disorder, and Mixed (or 'Schizoaffective') Psychosis," *Schizophrenia Bulletin*, vol. 35, no. 3, May 2009, pp. 482–490.

5. Ron Powers, *No One Cares About Crazy People*. New York: Hachette, 2017, p. 37.

6. E. Fuller Torrey, M.D., *Surviving Schizophrenia: A Family Manual, Sixth Edition*. New York: Harper Perennial, 2013, p. 125.

CHAPTER 2: HOW ARE PSYCHOTIC DISORDERS DIAGNOSED?

7. Quoted in Sylvia Nasar, *A Beautiful Mind: The Life of Mathematical Genius and Nobel Laureate John Nash*. New York: Simon & Schuster, 1998, p. 242.

8. Quoted in Nasar, *A Beautiful Mind*, p. 11.

9. Torrey, *Surviving Schizophrenia: A Family Manual,* p. 50.

10. Esmé Weijun Wang, *The Collected Schizophrenias: Essays*. Minneapolis, MN: Graywolf Press, 2019, p. 151.

11. David B. Arciniegas, "Psychosis," *Behavioral Neurology and Neuropsychiatry*, vol. 21, no. 3, June 2015, pp. 715–736.

12. Michelle Quilter, Psy.D. Personal interview. May 5, 2019.

13. Michelle Quilter, Psy.D. Personal interview. May 5, 2019.

14. Michelle Quilter, Psy.D. Personal interview. May 5, 2019.

15. Wang, *The Collected Schizophrenias*, p. 53.

16. Wang, *The Collected Schizophrenias*, p. 68.

17. Quoted in Moises Velasquez-Manoff, "When the Body Attacks the Mind," *Atlantic*, July/August 2016. www.theatlantic.com.

SOURCE NOTES CONTINUED

CHAPTER 3: WHAT IS LIFE LIKE WITH PSYCHOTIC DISORDERS?

18. George Manju, Shreemit Maheshwari, et al., "Understanding the Schizophrenia Prodrome," *Indian Journal of Psychiatry*, vol. 59, no. 4, October–December 2017, pp. 505–509.

19. Lily Fox. Personal interview. June 4, 2019.

20. Elyn R. Saks, *The Center Cannot Hold*. New York: Hyperion, 2007, p. 215.

21. Saks, *The Center Cannot Hold*, p. 215.

22. Saks, *The Center Cannot Hold*, p. 273.

23. Saks, *The Center Cannot Hold*, p. 276.

24. Wang, *The Collected Schizophrenias*, p. 70.

25. Wang, *The Collected Schizophrenias*, p. 72.

26. Quoted in Lynn Eleanor DeLisi, M.D., *100 Questions and Answers About Schizophrenia: Painful Minds, Third Edition*. Burlington, MA: Jones & Bartlett Learning Books, 2017, p. xxiii.

27. Torrey, *Surviving Schizophrenia: A Family Manual,* p. 127.

28. Ronald Chase. *Schizophrenia: A Brother Finds Answers in Biological Science*. Baltimore, MD: Johns Hopkins University Press, 2013, p. 124.

29. Lily Fox. Personal interview. June 4, 2019.

30. Powers, *No One Cares About Crazy People*, p. 260.

31. Powers, *No One Cares About Crazy People*, p. 202.

CHAPTER 4: HOW ARE PSYCHOTIC DISORDERS TREATED?

32. Quoted in DeLisi, *100 Questions and Answers About Schizophrenia: Painful Minds,* p. 57.

33. Eric R. Kandel, *The Disordered Mind: What Unusual Brains Tell Us About Ourselves.* New York: Farrar, Strauss and Giroux, 2018, p. 93.

34. Torrey, *Surviving Schizophrenia: A Family Manual,* p. 182.

35. Nicholas Tarrier and Rumina Taylor, "Schizophrenia and Other Psychotic Disorders," *Clinical Handbook of Psychological Disorders: A Step-by-Step Treatment Manual, Fifth Edition.* David H. Barlow (ed). New York: Guildford Press, 2014, pp. 506.

36. Tarrier and Taylor, "Schizophrenia and Other Psychotic Disorders," p. 507.

37. Tarrier and Taylor, "Schizophrenia and Other Psychotic Disorders," p. 507.

38. James Kelly and Patricia Gooding et al., "Intelligent Real-Time Therapy: Harnessing the Power of Machine Learning to Optimise the Delivery of Momentary Cognitive-Behavioural Interventions," *Journal of Mental Health,* vol. 21, no. 4, August 2012, pp. 404–414.

39. Shaun M. Eack, Gerard E. Hogarty, et al., "Cognitive Enhancement Therapy for Early Course Schizophrenia: Effects of a Two-Year Randomized Control Trial," *Psychiatric Services,* vol. 60, no. 11, November 2009, pp. 1468–1476.

FOR FURTHER RESEARCH

BOOKS

Ronald Chase, *Schizophrenia: A Brother Finds Answers in Biological Science*. Baltimore, MD: The Johns Hopkins University Press, 2013.

Lynn Eleanor DeLisi, M.D., *100 Questions and Answers About Schizophrenia: Painful Minds, Third Edition*. Burlington, MA: Jones & Bartlett Publishers, 2017.

Ron Powers, *No One Cares About Crazy People*. New York: Hachette, 2017.

E. Fuller Torrey, M.D., *Surviving Schizophrenia: A Family Manual, Sixth Edition*. New York: Harper Perennial, 2013.

Esmé Weijun Wang, *The Collected Schizophrenias: Essays*. Minneapolis, MN: Graywolf Press, 2019.

INTERNET SOURCES

"Early Psychosis and Psychosis," *National Alliance on Mental Illness*, 2019. www.nami.org.

"Psychotic Disorders," *MedlinePlus*, November 25, 2011. www.medlineplus.gov.

"Schizophrenia," *Mayo Clinic*, April 10, 2018. www.mayoclinic.org.

WEBSITES

American Psychiatric Association
www.psychiatry.org

This website is managed by a professional organization of psychiatrists. The website offers a plethora of solid information about all mental illnesses, psychotic disorders included.

American Psychological Association
www.apa.org/index

This website is managed by a professional organization devoted to psychology. It has useful information about psychotic disorders.

National Alliance on Mental Health
www.nami.org

NAMI is an advocacy group for those with mental illness. The website has lots of educational information to help individuals with mental illness and their families. The material provided is clear and concise.

National Institute of Mental Health
www.nimh.nih.gov/index.shtml

This is the website for the US governmental agency that researches mental health. The website is full of reliable and understandable information about all mental illnesses, including psychotic disorders. This website also offers links to relevant scientific articles.

World Health Organization
www.who.int

This website is managed by an organization that is concerned with health throughout the world. For a worldwide view of physical and mental illnesses, this is the place to visit.

INDEX

INDEX
CONTINUED

IMAGE CREDITS

ABOUT
THE AUTHOR

Marie-Therese Miller holds a Ph.D. in English from St. John's University. Miller and her husband, John, have five children and a grandson.